This book belongs to:

____

Made in the USA
Middletown, DE
05 January 2021

30822898R00062